PREDATOR vs. PREY

KOMODO DRAGONS vs. WILD BOARS

FOOD CHAIN FIGHTS

SARAH ROGGIO

Lerner Publications ◆ Minneapolis

To my nephew—wishing you many exciting adventures around the world!

Lerner Publications Company
An imprint of Lerner Publishing Group, Inc.
241 First Avenue North
Minneapolis, MN 55401 USA

For reading levels and more information, look up this title at www.lernerbooks.com.

Main body text set in Aptifer Sans LT Pro.
Typeface provided by Linotype AG.

Editor: Nicole Berglund **Photo Editor:** Nicole Berglund

Library of Congress Cataloging-in-Publication Data

Names: Roggio, Sarah, author.
Title: Komodo dragons vs. wild boars : food chain fights / Sarah Roggio.
Description: Minneapolis, MN : Lerner Publications, [2025] | Series: Predator vs. prey | Includes bibliographical references and index. | Audience: Ages 8–11 | Audience: Grades 4–6 | Summary: "Komodo Island is full of big Komodo dragons. But fierce wild boars can fight with their tusks. Readers learn how these creatures survive their environment, and each other. Then they decide who rules the island"— Provided by publisher.
Identifiers: LCCN 2024012807 (print) | LCCN 2024012808 (ebook) | ISBN 9798765647318 (lib. bdg) | ISBN 9798765662151 (pbk.) | ISBN 9798765656990 (epub)
Subjects: LCSH: Komodo dragon—Juvenile literature. | Wild boar—Juvenile literature. | Komodo dragon—Indonesia—Komodo Island—Juvenile literature. | Wild boar—Indonesia—Komodo Island—Juvenile literature. | Predation (Biology)—Juvenile literature.
Classification: LCC QL666.L29 R64 2025 (print) | LCC QL666.L29 (ebook) | DDC 597.95/968—dc23/eng/20240517

LC record available at https://lccn.loc.gov/2024012807
LC ebook record available at https://lccn.loc.gov/2024012808

Manufactured in the United States of America
1-1010994-53171-6/20/2024

TABLE OF CONTENTS

CHAPTER 1
CONFLICT ON KOMODO ISLAND

IT'S A WARM MORNING ON KOMODO ISLAND IN INDONESIA. This island is home to Komodo dragons. These reptiles are the largest lizards in the world! A Komodo dragon crouches behind a tamarind tree. Her body is big, but her brown skin blends in with the tree bark. Camouflage helps her hide

while she waits for prey. Over and over, she flicks her long, forked tongue. She uses her tongue to taste the air for the smell of nearby animals. She has been sitting in this same spot for hours.

Komodo dragons smell through their tongues instead of their noses.

At last! Three wild boars trot toward the tamarind tree. They are small prey for this gigantic dragon. The wild boars sniff the forest floor with their flat snouts. One of the boars uses his snout to scoop up a tamarind fruit. His two long tusks move up and down while he chews. He can use these two sharp tusks to defend himself from predators.

Different species of wild boars, such as this African giant forest hog, live all over the world.

KOMODO DRAGON STATS

AVERAGE TOTAL LENGTH: 10 feet (3 m) for males, 8 feet (2.4 m) for females

AVERAGE TAIL LENGTH: 5 feet (1.5 m) for males, 4 feet (1.2 m) for females

AVERAGE WEIGHT: 150 to 300 pounds (68 to 136 kg)

WILD BOAR STATS

AVERAGE TOTAL LENGTH: 3 to 6 feet (0.9 to 1.8 m)

AVERAGE TUSK LENGTH: 2 to 5 inches (5 to 13 cm)

AVERAGE WEIGHT: 110 to 200 pounds (50 to 91 kg)

Wild boars live for about ten years.

The wild boars hear a rustle behind the tree. Their heads jerk up, looking for danger. They grunt a loud warning to one another. Fear makes the stiff hairs on their backs stand up straight. This is another way the boars signal that danger is near.

The Komodo dragon hurries toward the male wild boar. Her body is massive, but she can move fast on her clawed feet. The boars flee. Will this wild boar be her meal? Let's find out!

Komodo dragons got their name because their tongues make it look as if they could breathe fire like dragons!

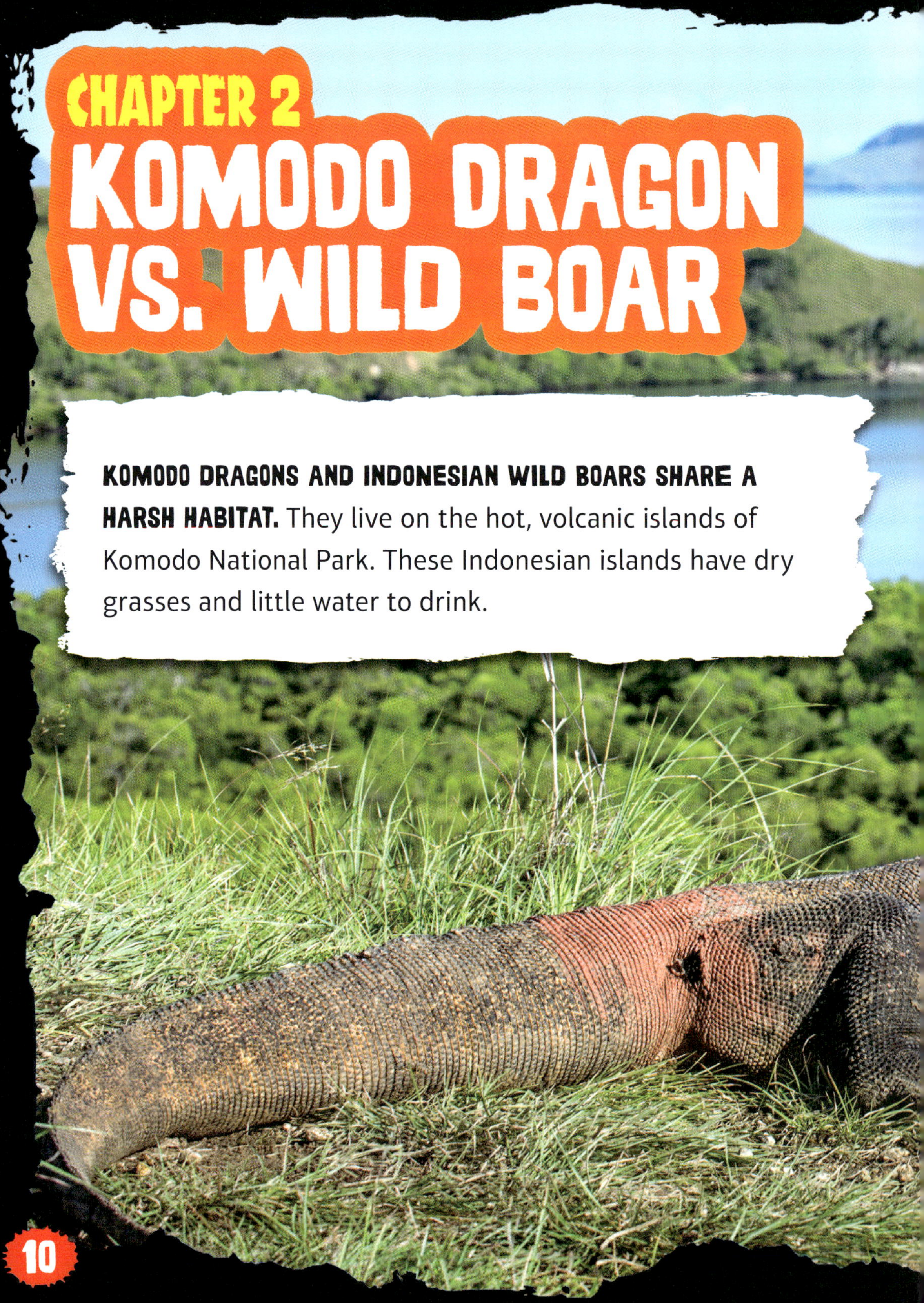

CHAPTER 2
KOMODO DRAGON VS. WILD BOAR

KOMODO DRAGONS AND INDONESIAN WILD BOARS SHARE A HARSH HABITAT. They live on the hot, volcanic islands of Komodo National Park. These Indonesian islands have dry grasses and little water to drink.

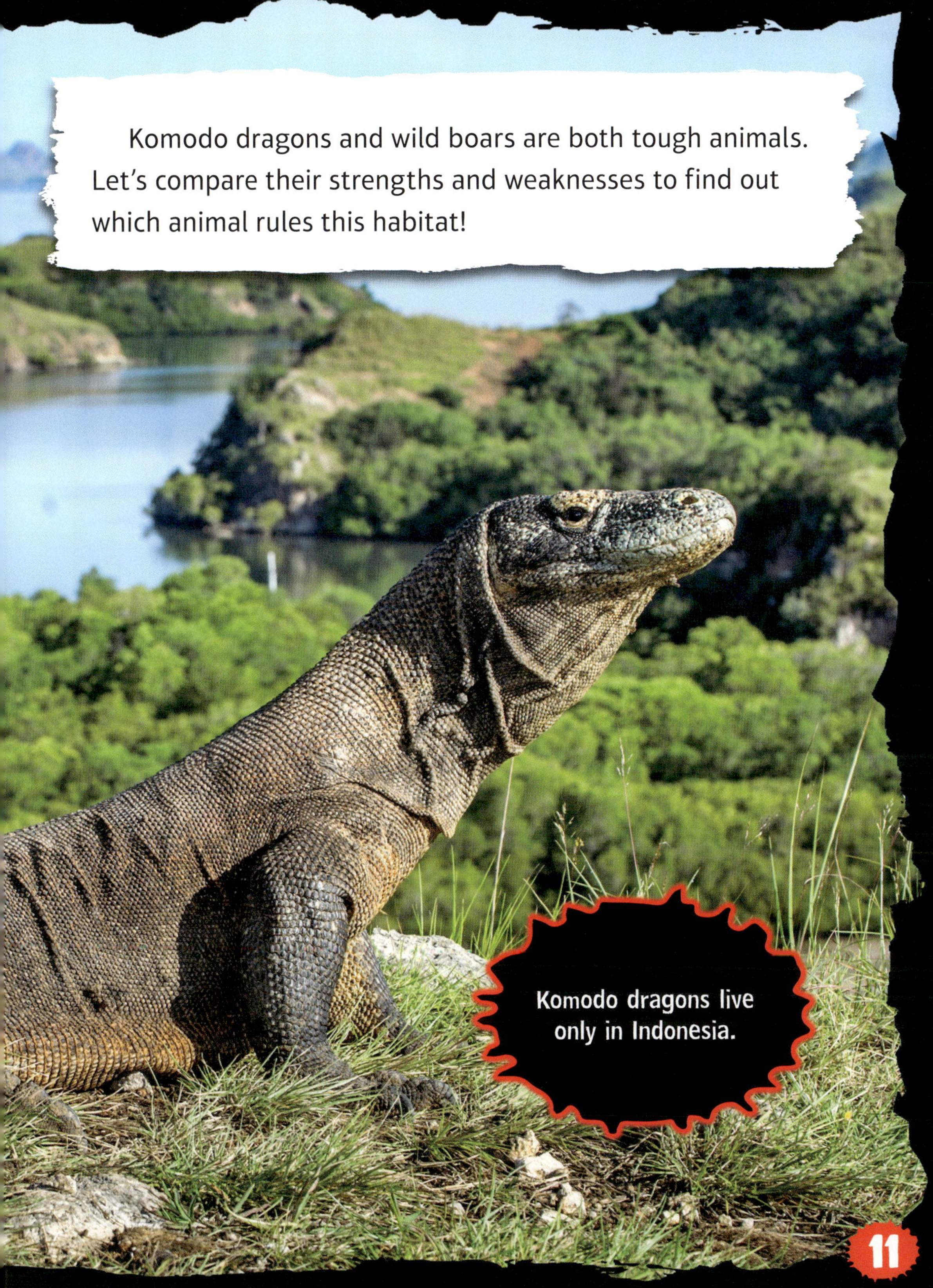

Komodo dragons and wild boars are both tough animals. Let's compare their strengths and weaknesses to find out which animal rules this habitat!

Komodo dragons live only in Indonesia.

A Komodo dragon eats a fish.

DIET AND HUNTING HABITS

Komodo dragons usually hunt alone. These carnivores eat anything from small birds to large water buffalo. They also scavenge for dead animals. Komodo dragons can eat up to 80 percent of their body weight in one meal!

KOMODO DRAGONS SMELL PREY FAR AWAY

Komodo dragons can use their forked tongues to smell prey up to about 5 miles (8 km) away.

Indonesian wild boars are omnivores. Like Komodo dragons, wild boars will scavenge for dead animals. But they also eat whatever else they can find. Their meals include berries, grass, insects, reptiles, and mice.

BABY BOARS ROOT RIGHT AWAY

Wild boar piglets learn how to root, or dig, for food as newborns. They start eating foods such as worms when they are about two weeks old.

Piglets search for food.

SIZE

Male Komodo dragons stand up on their two hind legs to fight. They can reach up to 8 feet (2.4 m) tall. This is more than 2 feet (0.6 m) taller than an average adult man!

Indonesian wild boars stand at about 2 feet (0.6 m) tall. Their piglets weigh 1.5 to 2 pounds (0.7 to 0.9 kg). But many other types of wild boar piglets weigh 2 to 4 pounds (0.9 to 1.8 kg). Indonesian wild boar adults weigh up to 418 pounds (190 kg). But other types of wild boars can weigh over 800 pounds (363 kg)!

Male Komodo dragons fight for land and mates.

Wild boars use their noses to search for food.

STRENGTH

Komodo dragons use their powerful tails to knock prey such as wild boars off their feet. Komodo dragons also have strong jaw and throat muscles. These muscles help them quickly swallow huge chunks of food.

Male wild boars have sharp tusks that grow to 6 inches (15 cm) long. During mating season, male wild boars fight by ramming each other with these tusks. They battle to see which boar will get to mate with a female boar.

KOMODO DRAGONS CAN DUMP WEIGHT

Komodo dragons with a full stomach can throw up their food to weigh less and run faster.

SPEED

Komodo dragons can run up to 13 miles (21 km) per hour. But they can't run fast for long, so prey often get away. That's why Komodo dragons usually wait for prey to come close to them.

Wild boars walk at 1 to 3 miles (1.6 to 4.8 km) per hour. But they can flee from predators at up to 30 miles (48 km) per hour. The fastest human ran at a top speed of 23 miles (37 km) per hour.

MOTHERS HIDE NEWBORN PIGLETS

Mother wild boars build nests for their piglets out of grass and dirt. These nests help them hide from predators on the ground.

A baby wild boar

Komodo dragons can live for more than thirty years!

AGILITY

Komodo dragons swing their bodies from side to side while walking. To run, they move their hind feet in a wide arc. These lizards fold their legs next to their body when swimming. They use their tail to propel them through the water.

Wild boars can walk slowly or trot at a medium speed. They can also gallop at high speeds. They can even jump up to 3 feet (0.9 m) to escape predators! Wild boars can also swim across rivers or other large bodies of water.

Each scale on a Komodo dragon contains a small bone.

ATTACK AND DEFENSE STYLES

Komodo dragons usually hide and wait for prey before launching an attack. Their goal is to bite an animal to kill it. To defend themselves, Komodo dragons have bony scales all over their bodies that act as armor. This armor protects them during battles with prey or other Komodo dragons.

STRIPES PROTECT BABY BOARS

Wild boar piglets are brown with black stripes until they are six months old. These colors help babies hide by blending in with their surroundings.

Mother wild boars live with their piglets in groups called sounders. These groups usually have two or three mothers and up to fifty piglets. The mothers protect their piglets by chasing away or biting predators.

KOMODO DRAGONS MAKE FAKE NESTS

Female Komodo dragons make real nests for their eggs on hills or in the ground. But they also dig fake nest holes to fool predators.

Similar to wild boars in the Netherlands (*above*), Indonesian wild boar sounders include mother wild boars and piglets.

KEY WEAPONS

Komodo dragons have good eyesight. They can see animals as far as 985 feet (300 m) away. Once prey gets close, Komodo dragons use their sharp teeth to attack. Prey die from the bacteria and venom in the dragons' saliva. The bacteria causes infections, and the venom causes blood loss. This harms the bodies of prey and causes them to slowly die.

POOP PROTECTS BABY KOMODO DRAGONS

Young Komodo dragons roll in poop so adult Komodo dragons won't eat them! Adult dragons don't like this smell and will leave these babies alone.

A Komodo dragon eye

Tusks help keep wild boars safe.

Sharp tusks are a male wild boar's best weapon. They use tusks to attack predators and other males. But male wild boars also have thick shoulder skin to protect themselves during fights. Female wild boars have sharp teeth to attack predators, but no tusks. All wild boars can kick with their hard hooves.

WEAKNESSES

Baby Komodo dragons can be meals for adult Komodo dragons! Baby Komodo dragons spend much of their first few years in trees. They hide there because adult dragons are too heavy to climb trees. Other baby Komodo dragon predators include wild boars, wild dogs, and snakes.

A baby Komodo dragon hides in the trees.

A wild boar walks through grass.

Wild boars are related to farm-raised pigs. Both animals are at risk of dying from swine fever. This disease killed many pigs on Flores, another Indonesian island, in 2021. Indonesian farmers are working to stop this disease from returning.

WILD BOARS DON'T SWEAT

Wild boars don't have sweat glands, so they stay cool by rolling in mud. Mud also protects their skin from pests such as lice.

CHAPTER 3
WHICH ANIMAL WILL WIN?

THE KOMODO DRAGON CATCHES UP TO THE MALE WILD BOAR. The two female boars scatter into the forest. The trapped male boar also tries to escape. But the Komodo dragon whips her powerful tail and sweeps his legs. The boar falls to the ground. He digs his feet into the dirt, trying to stand up again. The Komodo dragon dives toward the boar, ready to attack.

A Komodo dragon searches for prey.

But the boar strikes back. He jabs the Komodo dragon with his long tusks. He kicks the Komodo dragon with his hard hooves. Then he grunts and gets back on his feet. He snaps at the dragon with his sharp teeth. But he can't land a bite through this lizard's scaly skin.

The Komodo dragon circles the boar, saliva dripping from her mouth. She lunges and sinks her long fangs into the boar's neck. The bite is fatal. The boar is dying. The Komodo dragon waits until the boar stops moving. Then she eats her meal.

Venomous saliva drips from a Komodo dragon's mouth.

Wild boars watch for threats.

RULER OF THE HABITAT

Komodo dragons and wild boars are both fierce animals. Wild boars have sharp tusks and teeth to fight dragons. But Komodo dragons are big and strong. They can knock over wild boars with their muscular tails. Then they can kill boars with deadly bites.

The Komodo dragon won the battle. The wild boar tried to fight back, but the dragon was too powerful. Today, the Komodo dragon rules this island habitat.

PREDATOR VS. PREY: HEAD-TO-HEAD

KOMODO DRAGONS

- Forked tongue finds prey.
- Fangs deliver a deadly bite.

INDONESIAN WILD BOARS

- Sharp tusks jab and cut.
- Hard hooves kick attackers.

GLOSSARY

camouflage: how an animal hides by blending in with its habitat

carnivore: an animal that eats other animals

habitat: the place or type of place where a plant or animal normally lives or grows

mate: one in a pair of animals that comes together to produce young

omnivore: an animal that eats plants and other animals

predator: an animal that hunts other animals to eat

prey: an animal hunted by another animal for food

reptile: a cold-blooded animal whose babies often hatch from eggs

scavenge: to find and eat dead animals

volcanic island: an island formed as the result of volcanoes erupting

LEARN MORE

Britannica Kids: Indonesia
https://kids.britannica.com/kids/article/Indonesia/345708

Britannica Kids: Komodo Dragon
https://kids.britannica.com/kids/article/Komodo-dragon/390780

Gish, Melissa. *Komodo Dragons.* Mankato, MN: Creative Education and Creative Paperbacks, 2024.

Jackson, Tom. *Komodo Island and Other Places Ruled by Animals.* Minneapolis: Lerner Publications, 2024.

National Geographic Kids: Komodo Dragon
https://kids.nationalgeographic.com/animals/reptiles/facts/komodo-dragon

Wilson, Libby. *Wild Boars.* Mendota Heights, MN: Apex Editions, 2023.

INDEX

PHOTO ACKNOWLEDGMENTS

Image credits: Aprison Photography/Getty Images, pp. 4–5; Vicki Jauron, Babylon and Beyond Photography/Getty Images, p. 6; Nick Rains/Getty Images, p. 7 (top); Terry Allen/Alamy, pp. 7 (bottom), 29; pito kung/Getty Images, pp. 8, 15, 23, 27; Bruno Guerreiro/Getty Images, p. 9; USO/Getty Images, pp. 10–11, 28; Camptoloma/Shutterstock, p. 12; imageBROKER.com GmbH & Co. KG/Alamy, p. 13; ANDREYGUDKOV/Getty Images, pp. 14, 17; dwi septiyana/Getty Images, p. 16; FREEPIK2/Shutterstock, p. 18; WildT Animals/Alamy, p. 19; petesphotography/Getty Images, p. 20; christian_sutheja/Getty Images, p. 21; Anggo Hapsoro/Getty Images, p. 22; guenterguni/Getty Images, pp. 24–25; Michael Dunning/Getty Images, p. 26. Design elements: iunewind/Shutterstock; Milano M/Shutterstock; Cassel/Shutterstock; Textures and backgrounds/Shutterstock; Print Net/Shutterstock; Ukrainian studio/Shutterstock.

Cover: christian_sutheja/Getty Images; Riza Marlon/Getty Images.